JEHOVAH'S WITNESSES

A useful book for Jehovah's Witnesses,
friends, relatives, clergy and teachers

*All booklets are published thanks to the
generous support of the members of the
Catholic Truth Society*

CATHOLIC TRUTH SOCIETY
PUBLISHERS TO THE HOLY SEE

CONTENTS

INTRODUCTION

Dear Jehovah's Witness,

This booklet has been written mainly for you.

From my friendship with Jehovah's Witnesses for many years, I know that the ordinary member seeks to please God. You spend time studying Scripture. You attempt to lead a holy life. You do your best to witness about your beliefs to others. God certainly loves you for this.

The trouble is that, in spite of its claims, the Watchtower Society is not a trustworthy guide for salvation.

You have been given the New World Translation which is a corrupt version of Scripture.

The doctrines you are being taught contradict the full message of God's Word.

You are probably told not to read a booklet like this on the pretext that all criticism of Watchtower belief and practice is inspired by Satan, and that you should expect persecution by other Christians.

Please, give me a chance to speak to you so that we can work out the truth together. If what I say is wrong, the error will be apparent to you. *"Test everything; hold fast what is good, abstain from every form of evil"* (1 Thessalonians 5:21-22).

If you need more information, contact:

Christopher Wale,
212 Manstone Avenue,
Sidmouth,
Devon EX10 9TL.

He will be ready to speak to you. He also has a larger book for sale: *Contradictions. Jehovah's Witnesses versus the Bible* (380 pages; £ 7.00 incl. P&P). I made grateful use of this book in some of my chapters.

Why stay in darkness if you are called to walk in the light with Christ?

1. GOD'S NAME

What does the Watchtower Society teach?

Watchtower teachers say that God revealed his own personal name to be "Jehovah". They base this conviction on Exodus 3:13-15. As to the pronunciation "Jehovah", they derive this from the way in which the Hebrew word for God's name (YHWH - the *tetragammaton*= 'four-letter word') was transcribed in some classical English translations from the sixteenth century onward, notably the Authorised Version of 1611 (*Jehova* in four texts) and the American Standard Version of 1901. J.F. Rutherford, founder of the Jehovah's Witnesses who gave the movement its name, was not familiar with Hebrew, the language in which the oldest parts of Scripture were written.

In recent times, against the heavy odds of Hebrew scholarship, Watchtower spokesmen admit that they cannot be sure that "Jehovah" is the correct pronunciation of God's Name. However, they keep castigating Christians "for neglecting God's Holy Name".

They also contend that Jehovah (or its Hebrew equivalent) was the Name of God which Jesus came to manifest to his followers (see John 17:6).

1.1 What does Scripture say ?

In Old Testament times, God revealed himself to be "Yahweh" - "I AM WHO I AM". In the New Testament however, through the revelation of Jesus Christ, God revealed himself to be Father, Son and Holy Spirit.

1.1.1 God revealed himself in the Old Testament as 'I AM'

In the inspired Scriptures of the Old and New Testaments we do not find the name Jehovah even one single time. The name "Jehovah" is based on a great misunderstanding and on a lack of knowledge of ancient Hebrew and of Jewish practice.

God revealed his name to be "Yahweh", the meaning of which is expressed with reference to the Hebrew phrase: "Ehyeh asher ehyeh", which means: "I am who am".

But Moses said to God, "If I come to the people of Israel and say to them, 'The God of your fathers has sent me to you', and they ask me, 'What is his name?' what shall I say to them ?" God said to Moses, "I AM WHO AM". He also said, "Say this to the people of Israel, 'I AM has sent me to you'." God also said to Moses, "Say this to the people of Israel, 'Yahweh, the God of your ancestors, the God of Abraham, the God of Isaac, and the God of Jacob, has sent me to you': This is my name for ever, and thus I am to be remembered throughout all generations"
(Exodus 3:13-15; Revised Standard Version).

This text was written in Hebrew and people did not write vowels at the time. They only wrote consonants. God's name was therefore written as YHWH, the sacred *tetragammaton* = four letter word. Out of respect for God's Holy Name (Exodus 20:7), the Jews would not pronounce the name "Yahweh" when reading the text. They substituted the word "Adonai", (Lord) instead.

This was the custom also at Jesus' time and the time of the Apostles. Only from the fourth century after Christ did the Jews begin to write vowels under and above the consonants. With regard to the name Yahweh, however, they did not put the original vowels a-e, but inserted the vowels of "Lord", "Adonai": a-o-a. To ignorant people the word, therefore, looks like "Yahovah", which was then popularly changed to "Jehovah".

The original pronunciation of the word as "Yahweh" has been preserved in Hebrew names as an abbreviation; in the tradition of the Samaritans; with early Church Fathers such as Clement of Alexandria, Epiphanius and Theodoretus; and in other Greek transcriptions. Early Renaissance translators - Tyndale, Luther, etc. - wrote "Jehovah" because they did not have the means of reconstructing the original vocalisation of the tetragammaton. Most modern scholars accept that "Yahweh" is the correct pronunciation.

In actual fact, the word Yahovah or Jehovah did not exist. The Jews would say Adonai (Lord), knowing all the time that it stood for "Yahweh".

1.1.2 God revealed himself in the New Testament as 'Father'

In the scriptural tradition, a name stands for who a person is. While in the Old Testament God had revealed himself as I AM WHO AM, he continued that self revelation in the New Testament by revealing even more about himself.

Jesus manifested God as "the Father":

"I have made your name known to the people you took from

the world to give me" (John 17:6)
Jesus himself was manifested to us as "the Son":
"No one has ever seen God. It is the only Son, who is in the bosom of the Father, who has made him known"
(John 1:18).
"So that all may honour the Son as they honour the Father"
(John 5:23).
The Father and Jesus also manifested the Holy Spirit:
"The Counsellor, the Holy Spirit, whom the Father will send in my name, he will teach you all things" (John 14:26).
God, therefore, revealed himself to us in the Gospel under the new name "Father, Son and Holy Spirit":
"Go out and make disciples of all the nations, baptising them in the name of the Father and of the Son and of the Holy Spirit"
(Matthew 28:19).

1.2 The name 'the Lord'

Watchtower argument

In the old Hebrew Bible the name "Jehovah" appears 6823 times. In Christian Bibles God's name is suppressed and "the Lord" is used instead.

Response

Though God's name is printed as "Jehovah" in Hebrew Bibles, it stands for "Yahweh" and was pronounced as "Adonai", "Lord". The Greek translation of the Old Testament, the so-called Septuagint, completed by Jews in Alexandria in the 3rd century before Christ, followed the old Jewish custom. Out of respect for God's name "Yahweh", they translated it everywhere with *Kurios*, "Lord".

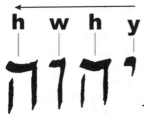

1. Hebrew characters were read from right to left. In the beginning only consonants were written. God's name, the sacred four-letter word, was written as YHWH, but pronounced as Yahweh

2. Out of respect for God's name, the Jews avoided reading it aloud. They began to substitute the word Adonai = 'Lord' in public readings. The four consonants are A-D-N-Y.

3. When vowel signs were added to the written text, as small signs below or above the consonants, the vowel signs of Adonai were placed on the consonants, of Jahoveh, to remember the substitution in reading.

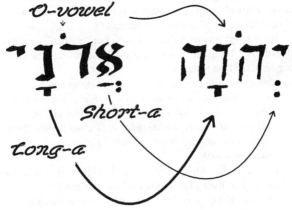

1.3 God as 'Father'

Watchtower argument

When Jesus taught us to pray, he made us call on God as Jehovah. "Pray in this way: 'Father Jehovah in heaven, hallowed be your name'." (Matthew 6:9).

It may be that the word "Jehovah" is not in the Gospel text here, but surely Jesus must have spoken the name of God fully. After all, he did not teach like the scribes and Pharisees (Matthew 7:29).

Response

Jesus taught us to say: "Our Father who art in heaven" (Matthew 6:9), or simply: "Father" (Luke 11:2). There is not a single passage in either the Gospels or in any other New Testament book in which God is addressed or spoken of as Jehovah. Is putting the name 'Jehovah' into Jesus' mouth not a typical distortion of a Gospel passage in Watchtower literature?

Jesus taught us to address God as our "Father", as "Dad" ("Dad" is "Abba" in Aramaic) because he reveals the loving person of God the Father to us.

"But when the fullness of time had come, God sent his Son, born of a woman, born under the law, in order to redeem those who were under the law, so that we might receive adoption as children. And because you are children, God has sent the Spirit of his Son into our hearts, crying, 'Abba! Father'!" (Galatians 4:4-6).

Jesus, as the Only Son of God, also had a personal relationship to the Father within God's divine nature.

"Father, glorify your Son, that the Son may glorify you...

Father, glorify me in your presence with the glory which I
had with you before the world was created" (John 17:1, 5)

The Lord Jesus Christ began everything, not in the name of
"Jehovah", but in the name of the Father. When he was praying,
it was to the Father. When he was teaching, he did so in the
name of the Father.

"Just as the Father knows me and I know the Father"
(John 10:15).
Jesus answered, "I have told you and you do not believe.
The works that I do in my Father's name testify to me"
(John 10:25).
And Jesus looked up and said, "Father, I thank you for
having heard me" (John 11:41).
Then Jesus, crying with a loud voice, said, "Father, into
your hands I commend my spirit". Having said this,
he breathed his last (Luke 23:46).

Jesus knew the expression 'the Lord God' as he shows when he
quotes Old Testament texts (Matthew 22:37; Luke 4:8). He himself
never called his Father "Jehovah". He simply called him "Father".

The new name of God which Jesus revealed to his followers
is: "Father" (John 17:6, 11).

1.4 Calling on Jesus as 'the Lord'

Watchtower argument

In the letter to the Romans 10:13, St Paul recalls the prophet
Joel 2:32, who states, "Everyone who calls on the name of
the Lord shall be saved". Since "the Lord" here surely means
Jehovah, it is clear from a New Testament text that we need
to call on the name Jehovah to be saved.

Response

The text does not mention Jehovah. It is true that in the Old Testament Hebrew text, the name YAHWEH was used. But the Apostles used the Greek so-called Septuagint version as their Scripture text, and this text carries *kurios*, "Lord".

The New World Translation, the Jehovah's Witnesses' version of Scripture, translates the word "Lord" about 200 times with "Jehovah" in the New Testament. There is absolutely no justification for this. Moreover, "the Lord" sometimes indicates the Father (Acts 4:24; 17:24), but usually it refers to Christ (Luke 2:11; 1 Corinthians 8:6; Revelation 17:14; 19:16; etc.).

For Paul, like for all early Christians, it is Jesus Christ who is "the Lord". Jesus Christ, as the Revealer of God to us, received what had been God's distinctive name in the Old Testament, the name YHWH = "the Lord".

"Therefore God highly exalted him and gave him the name that is above every name, so that at the name of Jesus every knee should bend, in heaven and on earth and under the earth, and every tongue should confess that Jesus Christ is Lord" (Philippians 2:9-10).

If the Name of Jesus is above all other names, it cannot be any other than the Name of God. Emphatically, this is stated in the Acts of the Apostles:

"Let it be known to all of you, and to all the people of Israel, that this man is standing before you in good health by the name of Jesus Christ of Nazareth, whom you crucified, whom God raised from the dead. This Jesus is 'The stone that was rejected by you, the builders; it has become the corner stone'. There is salvation in no one else for there is no other name under heaven given among mortals by which we must be saved" (Acts 4:10-12).

In the text quoted above (Romans 10:13), "calling on the name of the Lord" means "calling on the name of Jesus". Paul himself says so explicitly in the same passage, a few verses earlier: "If you confess with your lips that Jesus is Lord and believe in your heart that God raised him from the dead you will be saved" (Romans 10:9). It is by calling on Jesus as the Lord that we are saved.

1.5 Jesus is 'the Lord' also in heaven

Watchtower argument

The name of Jesus Christ may be the highest under heaven that is: on earth (see Acts 4:12). But the name "Jehovah" is the highest in heaven.

Response

In Philippians 2:9-10 it is clearly stated that Jesus received the highest name, the name of being the Lord, "in heaven, on the earth, and under the earth" (see above no 1.4). The Lord = *kurios* = *Adonai* = *Yahweh* is God's own name. In the New Testament it is Jesus' name. For Jesus is God, the revelation of God the Son.

Conclusion

God revealed himself as YAHWEH - I AM WHO AM in Old Testament times. But with the coming of Jesus Christ, God revealed an even more intimate name: Father, Son and Holy Spirit.

2. Jesus' Divinity

What does the Watchtower Society teach?

Watchtower teachers deny Jesus' divinity. Jesus, they say, lived
as a spirit person before he came to earth. He was God's first
creation, and so he is called the "firstborn" Son of God
(Colossians 1:15; Revelation 3:14). Jesus is the only Son whom
God created by himself. Jehovah used the prehuman Jesus as his
"master worker" in creating all other things in heaven and on
earth (proverbs 8:22-31; Colossians 1:16, 17). God also used
him as his chief spokesman. That is why Jesus is called "the
Word" (John 1:1-3; Revelation 19:13).

Jehovah's Witnesses are told that God sent his Son to the
earth by transferring his life to the womb of Mary. So Jesus did
not have a human father. That is why he did not inherit any sin
or imperfection. God sent Jesus to earth for three reasons: to
teach us the truth about God (John 18:37); to maintain perfect
integrity, providing a model for us to follow (1 Peter 2:21); and
to sacrifice his life to set us free from sin and death.

Jesus, they say, was a perfect human being just like Adam.
Unlike Adam, though, Jesus was perfectly obedient to God
under even the greatest test. He could therefore sacrifice his
perfect human life to pay for Adam's sin. This is what the Bible
refers to as the "ransom". Adam's children could thus be
released from condemnation to death. All who put their faith in

Jesus can have their sins forgiven and receive everlasting life (1 Timothy 2:5- 6; John 3:16; Romans 5:18-19).

When on earth, they say, Jesus cured the sick, fed the hungry, and calmed storms. He even raised the dead. Why did he perform miracles? He felt pity for people who were suffering, and he wanted to help them. His miracles proved that he was God's Son. They showed what he will do for obedient mankind when he rules as King over the earth.

The Watchtower says that after Jesus died, he was resurrected by God as a spirit creature, and he returned to heaven (1 Peter 3:18). Since then, God has made him a King, in 1914. Soon Jesus will remove all wickedness and suffering from this earth (Psalm 37:9-11; Proverbs 2:21-22).

2.1 What does Scripture say?

Scripture certainly attributes to Jesus Christ a very exalted position both among human beings and in heaven. This is where we agree with the Jehovah's Witnesses. But they miss the central message of Scripture with regard to Jesus Christ.

Jesus Christ was an extraordinary being, because he was both fully human and fully divine. This is what the Gospel expresses by saying that the Word (who is God) became flesh (see John 1:1; 1:14). See more about this Gospel verse in the next chapter, no 3.1.

According to his human nature, Jesus was, indeed, the firstborn of all creation (Colossians 1:14-15). Jesus was the new Adam, a "heavenly man" whose obedience brought us salvation from our sins (see 1 Corinthians 15:45-49; Romans 5:15-21). However, Jesus was more than just a human being or even than a spirit person in heaven.

Jesus, though human, was and is at the same time God. Jesus shares the divine nature with the Father and the Holy Spirit. These three "Persons" are one God. Sacred Scripture teaches this clearly, as will be shown in the chapter on the Blessed Trinity. Here we will focus on one key doctrine taught by Scripture, namely that Jesus is divine.

The Gospel shows that Jesus himself revealed his divine status. Jesus clearly taught:

- "I am God from all eternity with the Father".
- "I share all divine power with my Father".
- "I am the natural Son of God".

2.1.1 Jesus claimed to be God from all eternity with the Father

To facilitate the reading of the Gospel text, we will present it here in its original dramatic form. During the Feast of Tabernacles (cf. John 7:2, 14) Jesus had come to Jerusalem. He preached in the Temple. Directing the discussions to Jesus' own personality, the Jews began to challenge him (see John 8:52-58).

The Jews say: "Abraham is dead; the prophets are dead; and yet you say, 'If anyone obeys my teaching he shall not know what it is to die!' Are you greater than our Father Abraham, who is dead!? The prophets are dead too! What do you claim to be?" (Which means: Abraham was our greatest prophet and patriarch. But he also died. Do you claim to be greater than Abraham?) **Jesus says:** "Your Father Abraham was overjoyed to see my day. He saw it and was glad" (John 8:56). (Which means: Abraham, like all other Jews, was anxiously looking forward to the day when God was to redeem his people. This was called 'the Day of God'. Jesus calls it 'My Day', implying that he is God).

The Jews say: "You are not yet fifty years old. How can you have seen Abraham?"

Jesus says: "In very truth I tell you, before Abraham was, I AM" (John 8:58). (Which means: I have existed from all eternity. I Am Who AM".)

Here Jesus claims that he is the "I AM". Remember how God says to Moses: "when someone asks you, "Who is it that sends you?", say, "I AM sends me" (Exodus 3:13-14).

See about I AM WHO AM in chapter 1, no 1.1. It is clear from the Gospel that the Jews understood his claim to divine status. For they wanted to stone him (John 8:59). Stoning was the penalty for blaspheming against God (Leviticus 24:16).

Note that the New World Translation, the Jehovah's Witnesses' version of Scripture, deliberately mistranslates both passages. In Exodus 3:14 they translate: "I SHALL PROVE TO BE" instead of "I AM". In John 8:58 they translate "I HAVE BEEN" instead of "I AM". See next chapter about more such falsifications of Scripture!

The "I AM" statement was the strongest affirmation of God's identity in the Old Testament. We find it six times in Isaiah:

"I am Yahweh and outside me there is no other God!"
(Isaiah 45:5, 6 ,18 ,21 ,22; 46:9)

The expression I AM also stands on its own, expressing God's eternal being:

"Know and believe and understand that I AM. Before me no god was formed, nor shall there be any after me.
I, I am Yahweh. Apart from me there is no saviour"
(Isaiah 43:10-11).

In this light, Jesus' "I AM" claim can only be understood as a claim to be God:

"Before Abraham was, I AM" (John 8:58).

"You will die in your sins unless you believe that I AM" (John 8:24).

"When you have lifted up the Son of Man, then you will know that I AM" (John 8:28).

"That you may believe that I AM" (John 13:19).

Jesus claims, therefore, to be God himself, the God who appeared to Moses, the God who exists from all eternity, the I AM.

2.1.2 Jesus claimed to share all divine power
with the Father

On the occasion of Jesus' curing a paralytic in the pool of Bethesda, a dispute arose. Jesus had just said that he had the right to work on the Sabbath as God, his Father, was doing (John 5:18-23).

The Jews say: "You are not only breaking the Sabbath, but, by calling God your own Father, you claim equality with God!" (see John 5:18).

Jesus says: "The Son can do nothing by himself. He does only what he sees the Father doing" (John 5:19). (Which means: Surely, I am equal to the Father, but not as a second God next to him. The Father and I share the same divine nature). See chapter 4 on the Trinity, no 4.2).

Jesus says: "What the Father does, the Son does too" (John 5:19).

(a) "The Father loves the Son and shows him everything he does himself" (John 5:20).

(b) "As the Father raises the dead and gives them life, so the

Son gives life to people, as he determines" (John 5:21).

(c) "The Father does not judge anyone, but has given it to the Son to judge" (John 5:22).

(d) "So that all may honour the Son as they honour the Father" (John 5:23).

(This means: Only God knows everything. Only God can give life. Only God is the ultimate Judge. Only God deserves divine worship. This fourfold divine power is shared by Father and Son. The Son is absolutely equal to the Father, exercises the same divine activities and deserves the same honour).

Within the Blessed Trinity, the Father is the origin of everything. In that sense Scripture says that the Father *gives* everything to the Son. But it is a giving within God's own nature. That is why both Father and Son are (one) God.

Since Jesus as the Son proceeded from the Father, he refers to the Father as the one who sent him. This refers both to the divine mission within the Trinity and to Jesus' mission into the world as a human being.

Note also that Jesus proved his claim by a miracle. For the veracity of prophets was tested by the signs they gave.

The pool of Bethesda *(with its five colonnades)* was a water tank used for Temple purposes. Next to it was a Temple of the Greek God Asclepios, the god of health, and apparently there was a superstition that people were miraculously cured there. The paralytic was really not allowed to seek a cure in this pagan Temple. Jesus not only cured him, but forgave his sins, saying, "Leave your sinful ways" *(John 5:1-15; cf. vs. 14)*. Jesus appeals to the miracle as a proof of the veracity of his claim *(John 5:36-37)*.

Jesus says: "There is enough to prove to you that the Father has sent me, in the works my Father gave me to do: the very works *(miracles)* I am doing now. This is a proof given in my behalf by the Father who sent me, although you have never heard his voice or seen his form" (John 5:36-38).

In the Book of Deuteronomy the lawgiver *(Moses)* had given this rule to discern the true from the false prophet: "If you say to yourselves, 'How can we recognise a word which the Lord has not spoken?' - when a prophet speaks in the name of the Lord, if the word does not come to pass or come true, that is a word which the Lord has not spoken..." *(Deuteronomy 18:21-22)*. Jesus appeals to this rule *(John 5:41-47)*.

Jesus claims to be equal to the Father. He proves this claim by his miracles. The Jews should apply the rule laid down by Moses and judge him by the efficacy of his word.

2.1.3. Jesus is One with God the Father

On the feast of Dedication, during winter, Jesus had a discussion with the Jewish leaders in Solomon's Porch *(John 10:22)*. In the course of the conversation Jesus said "I and the Father are One." The Jews picked up stones to kill him *(John 10:31-39)*.

Jesus says: "I have done many good deeds before your eyes. I did these deeds with my Father's power. For which of these do you want to stone me?" (John 10:32).

The Jews say: "We are not going to stone you for any good deed, but for your blasphemy. You, a mere human being, claim to be God!" (John 10:33).

Jesus says: "Is it not written in your own Law, 'I said, you are gods'? Therefore, if those are called gods to whom the word of God is addressed and Scripture cannot be set aside! Then why do you charge me with blasphemy because I, consecrated

and sent into the world by the Father, said, 'I am God's son'?"
(John 10:34-36). (Which means: Do not be rash in your
judgement! You think that I am obviously a liar, because you
see that I am an ordinary human being and yet I claim to be God
at the same time. But a claim to 'be God' may be understood in
so many ways. In the Old Testament (Psalm 82:6) God calls
ordinary people 'gods' and surely for some good reason.
Therefore, take the trouble to find out in what way I claim to be
God's Son! Yes, I am human, but at the same time I share
God's nature with the Father.)

Jesus says: "If I were not acting as my Father would *(i.e. as
God would act)*, then do not believe me. But if I am, accept the
proof of my deeds - accept at least that much if you do not want
to believe me. Then you will recognise and admit that the Father
is in me and I in the Father" (John 10:37-38). (Which means:
God the Father and I are very intimately united. We are One
God ('The Father and I are One'). This you should realise,
considering that I am acting with divine power. You should at
least accept those proofs).

Note that, once more, Jesus proved his claim.

Jesus withdrew from Jerusalem. But very soon afterwards he
performed one of his greatest miracles: the raising of Lazarus
(John 11). This miracle symbolised Jesus' power to give life *(as
only God can do)* and prepared the way for Jesus' Resurrection.
This last sign clearly proved to many Jews that Jesus could only
be working with God's sanction:

> *"Now many of the Jews who had come to visit Mary, and
> who had seen what Jesus did [raising Lazarus from the
> dead], put their faith in him" (John 11:45).*

> *"A great number of Jews heard that Jesus was there [in
> Bethany], and came not only to see Jesus, but also Lazarus*

whom he had raised from the dead. The chief priests then resolved to do away with Lazarus as well, since on his account many Jews were going over to Jesus and putting their faith in him" (John 12:9-11).

"The people who were present when he called Lazarus out of the tomb and raised him from the dead told what they had seen and heard. That is why the crowd went to meet him. They had heard of this sign that he had performed" (John 12:17-18).

From all these passages it is clear that Jesus himself revealed his divine status. Jesus clearly taught:

- "I am God from all eternity with the Father".
- "I share all divine power with my Father".
- "I am the natural Son of God".

2.2 Jesus' eternal existence as God

Watchtower argument

In John 8:58, when Jesus says: "Before Abraham ever was, I am", it does not prove his divinity. The expression used is different from the I AM in Exodus 3:14. Moreover, in John 8:58 Jesus' debate with the Jews concerned his age. Jesus claimed no more than pre-human existence, as a spirit person in heaven. The Jews wanted to stone Jesus for claiming to have seen Abraham, not for claiming to be God.

Response

Jesus' debate with the Jews did involve his eternity, but this was more than just a question of pre-human existence. Jesus claimed eternity with the Father. This implied equal divinity with the Father.

Moreover, the Greek expression I AM (**ego eimi**) in John 8,58 is exactly the same as in the official Jewish Greek translations of Exodus 3:14 (**ego eimi**) and in Is 43:10-11 (**ego eimi**). It is the direct translation of the Hebrew I AM (**ehyeh**). No one could miss the fact that Jesus by this title clearly claimed to be God himself, especially since Jesus used it many times (see also John 8:24; 8:28; 13:19).

The Gospel states explicitly that the Jews understood the claim:

"The Jews were intent on killing Jesus, because, not content with breaking the Sabbath, he spoke of God as his own Father, and so made himself God's equal" (John 5:18).

"We are not stoning you for doing a good work, but for blasphemy. You are only a human being and you claim to be God!" (John 10:33).

Claiming to have lived before Abraham did not deserve the death penalty in the eyes of the Jews. Claiming to be equal to God did.

2.3 'No one is good except God'

Watchtower argument

When the rich young man came to Jesus he asked: "Good Master, what must I do to win eternal life?" Jesus replied: "Why do you call me good' No one is good except GOD alone!" (Mark 10:17-18). Jesus himself therefore declared that he was not God.

Response

It was not the custom to add "good" to the Jewish title 'Master' *(which was Rabbi, Rabboni in Hebrew)*. 'Good Master' was a specially flattering way of speaking, as when someone would address a priest as "kind Father". In his reply to the young man, Jesus shows that he does not like this type of flattery. That is why he says to him: "Why do you call me good?"

Jesus adds: "No one is good except God alone". Jesus does not mean literally that we cannot call anyone good except God, for he himself speaks of 'good people' on other occasions *(Matthew 5:45; 12:35; 20:15; 22:10; etc.)*. Jesus wants to say that strictly speaking all goodness comes from God. The young man certainly did not realise to what extent Jesus could be called good.

This passage in the Gospel reminds me of an incident I once read about. A famous American scientist visited an Italian Museum. The guide - who had no idea to whom he was speaking - was addressing the American time and again as "excellenza". The man got irritated and asked: "Why do you call me 'excellenza'?! Only famous people are called 'excellenza'!" He did not want to deny that he was well known *(famous)* as a scientist, but he could not bear to be flattered like that by a man who did not know him!

Jesus' reaction was similar to this. Jesus does not deny that he can be called good and that he himself is God, but he wants the young man to reflect on the *meaning* of 'being good'. In this way he wants to draw him on to acknowledge his divinity.

When the Apostle Thomas knelt before Jesus, after the resurrection, with the words: "my Lord and my God!" *(John 20:28)*, Jesus did not stop him. He never stopped people who sincerely confessed their faith in his divinity *(see also Matthew 16:16)*.

2.4 Jesus and the Father

Watchtower argument

At the Last Supper Jesus prayed with these words: "This is eternal life: to know you who alone are truly God and Jesus Christ whom you have sent" (John 17:3). Would it not seem from Jesus' words that he distinguishes the only true God from himself? Does he thereby not deny to be God?

Response

Jesus distinguishes between the Father and himself as two persons within God, but as regards divinity he puts both on the same level.

To gain eternal life one has to know both the Father and the Son! How do we know them? In two stages: by natural revelation *(by which we know the Father as the only true God, i.e. by considering creation)* and by the supernatural revelation of Jesus *(by which we know the Son, who was sent by the Father).* Jesus' words mean therefore: Eternal life will be given to those who accept both revelations, that is: who accept the Father as Creator of the world and the Son as Revealer of the Trinity. With these words he does not deny his divinity; rather, he teaches his divinity through them.

This is also obvious if we read the whole prayer contained in John 17. Jesus says, for instance:

"Father, glorify me in your own presence with the glory which I had with you before the world began" (John 17:5).

God's glory is exclusively God's. Jesus is asking the Father to manifest the divine glory which he, Jesus, possessed with the Father from all eternity! Surely, he could not express his claim to divinity in more convincing terms!

2.5 'Jesus grew in wisdom'

Watchtower argument

Jesus grew up as a small boy in Nazareth. We read: "As Jesus grew up he advanced in wisdom and in favour with God and people" *(Luke 2:52)*. If Jesus was God, how could he advance in wisdom?

Response

We should not forget that Jesus was truly human at the same time. He was like us in all aspects. He ate like us; he worked like us; he was tired like us. When he was beaten he suffered and felt pain, just as we would. His appearance to other people was like any human person. Jesus also could acquire knowledge as ordinary people do.

We are touching the mystery of the Incarnation here, the 'emptying himself of equality with God', as Paul calls it (Phil 2:6-7). We do not fathom the ins and outs of Jesus' psychology. We can only guess.

Things he knew in his divinity, could yet be learned by his humanity. It is quite a different thing to possess infinite knowledge as God and to store newly acquired knowledge in the human memory. In this way Jesus could truly be said to advance in wisdom. As God Jesus possessed everything; yet as a human being he received gifts from other human beings.

Conclusion

Jesus claimed divine status. He claimed equality with the Father. From that we know that he shares all divine powers

with the Father. Together with the Father and the Holy Spirit, he is God.

Jesus is, at the same time, human.

This mystery is directly expressed by Scripture in texts such as these:

"The Word was God... And the Word became flesh"
(John 1:1, 14).

"He is the image of the unseen God, the first-born of all creation, for in him were created all things in heaven and on earth... Before anything was created, he existed"
(Colossians 1:15-17).

"For in him the whole fullness of deity dwelt bodily"
(Colossians 2:9).

To escape the clear teaching of such passages, the Watchtower Society has falsified its translation of Scripture. See the next chapter about this.

3. SACRED SCRIPTURE

What does the Watchtower Society teach?

The Watchtower leaders hold out the Bible as the unerring word of God and claim to base all of their teachings directly on Scripture. They promote Scripture study among their members. They quote Scripture when recruiting disciples. They maintain that they are the only 'Christian' group that truly understands and honours God's Word.

If such is the case, the accuracy and reliability of the Scripture text used is of paramount importance. After all, what use is an English text, if it is not an exact statement of the original and so distorts God's message?

The Governing Body of the Jehovah's Witnesses brought out its own translation of Sacred Scripture in 1950 which is known as the **New World Translation**. It has been reprinted many times since.

The work is presented as an accurate translation of the biblical text. "We offer no paraphrase of the Scriptures. Our endeavour all through has been to give as literal a translation as possible, where the modern English idiom allows and where a literal rendition does not for any clumsiness hide the thought" (NWT of the Christian Greek Scriptures, 1950, p.9).

The sad truth is that the New World Translation, on which Jehovah's Witnesses now routinely rely, is a text in which the inspired message has been deliberately mistranslated. The translation is corrupt, full of mistranslations and deceptions, a betrayal of God's sacred inspired Word.

This is all the more irresponsible and contemptible since so many sincere Jehovah's Witnesses depend on this translation for their eternal salvation.

We will demonstrate the deceitfulness at the hand of ten passages relating to Jesus Christ in which the New World Translation has intentionally changed the text in order to disprove the divinity of Christ. (For each of the following passages I will first print a correct translation (RSV: Revised Standard Version), then the version presented by the New World Translation (NWT).)

3.1 John 1:1

"In the beginning was the Word, and the Word was with God, and the Word was God." (RSV)
"Originally the Word was, and the Word was with God, and the Word was a god." (NWT)

The context of this passage shows that the Word refers to Jesus Christ. "The Word became flesh and dwelt among us", etc. (John 1:14). The text therefore strongly affirms Jesus' divinity. "The Word is God."

The Watchtower Society justifies the NWT version "the Word was a god" on the grounds that the original Greek here has "god" without an article: *theos*, not *ho theos*. The translation however is wrong for the following reasons:

• In Greek the article is often omitted when it is the predicate of the verb 'to be'. Like in English, Greek people would say: "Elizabeth is Queen", meaning "Elizabeth is *the* Queen".

• Greek scholars agree on this. In spite of Watchtower claims, no Greek scholar agrees with their translation of John 1:1.

• In the New Testament the word *theos* occurs 1303 times referring to God. There are 220 cases where *theos* does not carry the article and yet clearly means God (not a god). In those cases the NWT also translates *God*.

• The translation "a god" makes no sense applied to Jesus. Are there small "gods" next to "God"? On the contrary, the whole passage (John 1:1-18) shows Jesus' divinity: his eternity, his creative work, his act of salvation, his glory. This is also affirmed in the last verse:

• "No one has ever seen God; the only begotten God who is in the bosom of the Father, he has made him known" (John 1:18). In line with their bias against Jesus' divinity, the NWT renders as follows: "No one has seen **God** at any time; the only begotten **god** who is in the bosom with the Father is the one that has explained him".

3.2 John 8:58

"Before Abraham was, I am." (RSV)
*"Before Abraham came into existence, **I have been**." (NWT)*
The original Greek says: "ego eimi", that is: "I am". There is no justification for changing the verb into "I have been".

Jesus' I AM statement, which he repeats four times (John 8:24, 28, 58; 13:19), link up with God's own name I AM (see Exodus 3:14; Is 43:10-11). It clearly proves that Jesus claimed divinity (see previous chapter, no 2.1.1).

3.3 John 17:5

"Father, glorify me in your presence with the glory which I had with you before the world was made." (RSV)

*"Father, glorify me **alongside** yourself with the glory that I had **alongside** you before the world was made." (NWT)*

Throughout John's Gospel Jesus proclaims that he shares divinity with the Father: eternal existence, knowledge, the power to give life, judgement and worship (see chapter 2, no. 2.1.2). This is also implied here. Jesus shared the Father's divine glory from all eternity. The NWT wants to suggest that Jesus is of a lower status.

3.4 Romans 9:5

"Of their race, according to the flesh, is the Christ, who is God over all, blessed for ever. Amen." (RSV)

"From whom Christ [sprang] according to the flesh: God who is over all, [be] blessed for ever." (NWT)

The NWT translation is possible here, if we assume a sudden break in the sentence. But it disrupts the flow of the Greek text. Does the NWT not translate the way it does to avoid having to join "God" to Christ? Read the parallel text of Romans 1:3-4: "descended from David according to the flesh and designated Son of God in power according to the Spirit of holiness by his resurrection from the dead, Jesus Christ our Lord" (RSV).

3.5 Romans 10:13

"For everyone who calls on the name of the Lord will be saved." (RSV)

*"For everyone who calls on the name of **Jehovah** will be saved." (NWT)*

The Watchtower leaders refuse to accept that Jesus too can be called upon as God. They justify the above translation saying that the text is quoted from Joel 2:32 where the Hebrew has Jahweh.

The translation is wrong:

• In the same passage Paul makes clear that Jesus is 'the Lord': "If you confess with your lips that Jesus is Lord and believe in your heart that God raised him from the dead, you will be saved" (Romans 10:9). Confessing that Jesus is Lord is calling on the name of the Lord
(see also chapter 1, no 1.4).

• Jesus is 'Jahweh', the Lord, for the early Christians (see Philippians 2:5-11; 1 Corinthians 8:6; Luke 2:11; Revelation 17:14; 19:16; etc.).

• Jesus' name is above all other names in heaven, on the earth and under the earth (Philippians 2:9; Ephesians 2:21). "There is no other name under heaven given among people by which we must be saved" (Acts 4:12).

3.6 Colossians 1:16-17

"He is the image of the invisible God, the firstborn of all creation; for in him all things were created, in heaven and on earth, visible or invisible... All things were created through him and for him. He is before all things, and in him all things hold together." (RSV)

"He is the image of the invisible God, the firstborn of all creation; by means of him all other things were created in the heavens and upon the earth, the things visible and the

*things invisible... All other things were created through him
and for him. He is before all other things, and in him all
other things hold together." (NWT)*

Four times the NWT adds the word "other" in order to imply
that Jesus himself was also a created thing, namely the 'firstborn
of creation'. The word "other", however, is not found in the
Greek text. Jehovah's Witnesses justify this addition, saying
that it is demanded by the context - meaning they refuse to
accept that Scripture says that Jesus was Creator and himself
uncreated.

The change of the text is wrong:

• The 'all creation' following 'firstborn' is a comparative
genitive. 'Firstborn of all creation' means, therefore, *'earlier
than* all creation, *before* all creation'. In the same way we
read: "he was the *first of me*" meaning "he was before me"
(John 1:15); "the world hated me first of you", that is:
"the world hated me before you" (John 15:18).

• This meaning is confirmed by the next verses where Paul
repeatedly and explicitly states that Jesus created **everything**
(ta panta), that he was before everything, that everything
was created through him and for him (Colossians 1:15-17).

• The same is affirmed in the Gospel. Jesus, as the Word, as
Son of God, was the universal Creator. "All things *(ta panta)*
were made through him, and without him was not made
anything that was made" (John 1:3). Jesus stood outside
creation. He was not one creature like 'other' creatures.

3.7 Colossians 2:9

*"For in him (Christ) the whole fullness of deity dwells
bodily"* (RSV)

*"For in him (Christ) the fullness of **the divine quality** dwells
bodily"* (NWT).

The word in the Greek text is *theotes* (= "deity", "divinity"),
not *theiotes* (= "divineness", divine quality"). *Theotes* was a
well known concept among Greek writers of the time. It always
denotes 'being God', 'the essence of God'. The NWT falsifies
the meaning by its translation.

The original text teaches clearly that the whole (!) fullness of
Godhead dwells in Jesus Christ bodily, a wonderful parallel to:
"The Word became flesh" (John 1:14). Paul repeats the teaching
in Colossians 1:19: "For in him all the fullness [of God] was
pleased to dwell".

3.8 Titus 2:13

*"Awaiting our blessed hope, the appearing of the glory of
our great God and Saviour Jesus Christ."* (RSV)

*"Awaiting our blessed hope, the appearing of the great God
and of (the) Saviour of us, Jesus Christ."* (NWT)

The NWT translates this verse as if God and Jesus Christ are
separated. However, the normal sense of the Greek text states,
in one breath: 'the great God and Saviour Jesus Christ'. Here
are the reasons why:

• There is no definite article before 'Saviour'. This means the
two nouns are joined by the same article.

• The following verse, Colossians 2:14, is a relative clause
which has only one subject, namely Jesus Christ.

•"God and Saviour" is a joint title, frequently used in ancient
literature of the same time.

•The appearing *(epiphaneia)* mentioned in the verse is
always Jesus' appearance (2 Thessalonians 2:8; 1 Timothy
6:14; 2 Timothy 1:10; 2 Timothy 4:1, 8).

•It is confirmed by the parallel texts: "our God and Saviour
Jesus Christ" (1 Peter 1:1) and "the Lord and Saviour Jesus
Christ" (2 Peter 1:11; 2:20; 3:18).

3.9 Revelation 3:14

*"The words of the Amen, the faithful and true witness, the
beginning of God's creation." (RSV)*
"The words of the Amen, the faithful and true witness,
the beginning of the creation by God." (NWT)
The NWT here interprets the expression as if it implies that
Jesus himself was created. This is wrong for the following
reasons:

•The beginning *(arche)* of creation should be understood in
the same way as the 'firstborn of all creation', namely in the
sense of his coming *before* creation (see no 3.6). In this
sense Jesus is called the beginning *(arche)* in Colossians
1:18, as the one who created everything and who existed
before any created thing existed (Colossians 1:15-17).
Modern translations, therefore, render the phrase as
"the ultimate source of God's creation" (Jerusalem Bible),
"the origin of all that God has created" (Today's English
Version), "the prime source of all God's creation"
(New English Bible).

- The proclamation of Jesus as 'the beginning' implies his
divinity. For God himself is 'the First and the Last' (Is
44:6.8; 48:12). God is the 'Alpha and Omega' (= first and
last letters of the alphabet; Revelation. 1:8). But Jesus too is
'the First and the Last': "I am the First and the Last"
(Revelation 1:17); "So speaks the First and the Last"
(Revelation 2:8); "Behold, I am coming soon .... I am the
Alpha and the Omega, the First and the Last, the beginning
and the end" (Revelation 22:12-13).

3.10 Proverbs 8:1-36

*"Does not wisdom call? Does not understanding raise her
voice? On the heights beside the way, in the paths she takes
her stand.... The Lord created me at the beginning of his
work, the first of his acts of old.... When he marked out the
foundations of the earth, I was beside him like a master
workman..." (Proverbs 8:1-2, 22, 30; RSV)*

*"Does not wisdom keep calling out, and discernment keep
giving forth its voice? On top of the heights, by the way, at
the crossing of the roadways it has stationed **itself**....
Jehovah himself produced me as the beginning of his way,
the earliest of his achievements of long ago... When he
decreed the foundations of the earth, then I came to be
beside him as a master worker..."*
(Proverbs 8:1-2, 22, 30; NWT)

The NWT has translated wisdom in a neutral sense, as 'it',
'itself', etc. Why? You may ask. And is it important? The
answer is: yes. For Jehovah's Witnesses apply this text to Jesus
Christ. They use this passage as their main Scripture text to
prove that Jesus was created by God (as wisdom was), that he

was a spirit creature in heaven and that he was the 'master worker' by means of whom God created everything else.

About this interpretation, note the following:

•Proverbs 8:1-36 presents wisdom as a woman. Not only is the word 'wisdom' *(chokmah)* feminine; the text uses feminine pronouns ('she', 'herself', 'her') throughout. This is consistent with the figure of wisdom in Proverbs who is always presented as a *female teacher*. See Proverbs 1:20-33; 7:4; 9:1-6. The NWT deliberately changed this picture for Proverbs 8:1-36 because it was realised that wisdom as a female teacher does not fit well as a figurative description of Jesus.

•There is absolutely no scriptural basis for reading in this text doctrinal information about Jesus. The text is not quoted in the New Testament. It simply tells us that God created everything with wisdom - God's wisdom being personified as a woman.

Conclusion

In ten clear instances I have shown that Jehovah's Witnesses are given a corrupt version of Scripture. In all ten examples the text has been deliberately twisted and perverted to give the impression that Jesus is not God. Some words are added, others omitted and others bent around to suit Watchtower doctrine.

Elsewhere in this booklet I will show that a similar habitual distortion of Scripture occurs when other points of doctrine are concerned.

Tampering with the Word of God is a serious offense. It misleads those who are sincerely seeking to know what God has revealed and who do not have the opportunity to check the translation against the original Hebrew and Greek Scriptures.

"You shall not add anything to the word I command you, nor take anything from it!" (Deuteronomy 4:2)

"I warn everyone who hears the prophecy of this book: If anyone adds to them, God will add to him the plagues described in this book; and if anyone takes away from the words of the book of this prophecy, God will take away his share in the tree of life and in the holy city which are described in this book." (Revelation 22:18-19)

God be merciful to those who produced the New World Translation and to the Watchtower authorities who recommend it as a faithful rendering of Scripture.

4. FATHER, SON AND SPIRIT

What does the Watchtower Society teach?

The Watchtower says that the doctrine of the Holy Trinity cannot be found in Sacred Scripture. Nor was it part of the Christian faith during the first three centuries after Christ. Belief in the Blessed Trinity was only introduced into Christianity during the course of the fourth century, they maintain, in imitation of the many trinitarian pagan divinities.

According to Watchtower doctrine, belief in Father, Son and Holy Spirit contradicts belief in One God, never mind the usual Christian excuses. The assertion that the Blessed Trinity is a mystery transcending human understanding is dismissed as an admission of utter inability to make sense of a self-contradictory absurdity.

What does Scripture say?

The Old Testament teaching about God is much richer and more mysterious than the Watchtower interpretation implies.

The insistence on belief in one God - "Yahweh our God is Yahweh alone" (Deuteronomy 6:4); "You shall have no other gods before me" (Exodus 20:3), was not a numeric statement about organic unity in God, but rather a polemical statement against pagans. It taught that God was different from the multiplicity of nature gods (sun, moon, animals, and so on) worshipped by pagans (Deuteronomy 4:15-19).

Even in the Old Testament, God revealed different aspects of his being: the Spirit, the Lord of Hosts, the God Most High, Wisdom, and so on. The ordinary word used for 'God' in the Old Testament (2300 times) is the Hebrew word *Elohim*, which is a plural word. Literally it means 'Gods'. Of course, it is a so-called 'plural of majesty' - but does it not show that the 'One God' has a more complex and mysterious inner reality than numerical oneness?

Jesus Christ who came to us from within the mystery of God, revealed to us intimate information about who God is. God is Father, Son and Holy Spirit. Although it is a belief difficult to grasp in human thought and difficult to express in human words, it provides us with an exciting new insight into the interior life of God.

We will review the Scriptural message in two steps:
- Jesus revealed God to us as Father, Son and Holy Spirit.

- Scripture mentions Father, Son and Holy Spirit together as pertaining to the One reality of God.

4.1 Jesus revealed God to us as Father, Son and Holy Spirit

Jesus revealed God to us as "Father". Whereas God, in Old Testament times, made himself known to us as the "I AM", as "I AM WHO AM", Jesus revealed to us that the deepest origin in God should be understood as "Father". Jesus taught us to call God no longer by the Old Testament name, but by his own appellation "Dad", "Abba", "Father" (see chapter 1, no 1.1.2).

Jesus also revealed himself as the Son. As the first born Son of the Father, he was in the bosom of the Father from all eternity. He shares divine life with his Father.The Father and the Son share their infinite knowledge, their creative power, their judgement over good and evil and their right to worship. Whatever the Son has, he has received from all eternity within the Godhead from the Father (see chapter 2, no 2.1.2).

Jesus also revealed to us the Holy Spirit. Whereas even in the Old Testament the spirit of God was known as the power that gave life and inspired prophets, Jesus revealed to us that "the Holy Spirit" too shares in the divine life with the Father and the Son. This is a new revelation that goes much beyond the Old Testament understanding of God's life-giving spirit.

"The Counsellor, the Holy Spirit, whom the Father will send in my name, he will teach you all things" (John 14:26).

"When the Counsellor comes, whom I shall send to you from the Father, even the Spirit of Truth, who proceeds from the Father he will bear witness to me" (John 15:26).

Just as the Son shares all divine life and power with the Father, so the Son shares all divine life and power with the Spirit.

• Like the Son, the Spirit is sent by the Father (John 14:26) and comes into the world (John 16:7, 13).

• As the Son is the Holy One of God (John 6:69), the Spirit is the *Holy* Spirit (John 14:26).

• As the Son is the *Truth* (John 14:6), the Spirit is the Spirit of Truth (John 14:13).

• Only believers will know and see the Holy Spirit (John 14:17), as only believers will know and see the Son (John 14:19-20).

• The Holy Spirit lives in the disciples (John 14:17), as the Son lives in them (John 14:20; 15:4).

Jesus therefore showed us that Father, Son and Holy Spirit are God: that Father, Son and Holy Spirit share the divine life in a dynamic mutual relationship of which we, human beings, can only have a glimpse.

4.2 Sacred Scripture presents Father, Son and Holy Spirit as pertaining together to the One reality of God

In the New Testament, Father, Son and Holy Spirit are often mentioned in the same verse within the context of the Godhead.

4.2.1 It is Father, Son and Holy Spirit who together saved us in the work of redemption

"Chosen and destined by God the Father and sanctified by the Spirit for obedience to Jesus Christ and for sprinkling with his blood" (1 Peter 1:2).

4.2.2 Baptism is the Christian ritual through which we become the adopted children of God

Baptism should, however, not be administered in the name revealed in the Old Testament "I AM", but in the newly revealed name of God "Father, Son and Holy Spirit".

"Go therefore and make disciples of all nations, baptising them in the name of the Father and of the Son and of the Holy Spirit" (Matthew 28:19).

4.2.3 God is present in the life of every Christian

After Jesus' revelation of the new relationships within God, we now know that Father, Son and Holy Spirit are all active within us.

"There are varieties of gifts, but the same Spirit; and there are varieties of service, but the same Lord; and there are varieties of workers, but it is the same God who inspires them all in everyone."(1 Corinthians 12:4-6).

"But it is God (the Father) who establishes us with you in Christ, and has commissioned us; he has put his seal upon us and given us his Spirit in our hearts as a guarantee" (2 Corinthians 1:21-22).

4.2.4 After Jesus' revelation of who God is, our Christian blessing will incorporate Father, Son and Holy Spirit

"The grace of the Lord Jesus Christ and the love of God (the Father) and the fellowship of the Holy Spirit be with you all" (2 Corinthians 13:14).

4.2.5 Our Christian prayers will now involve Father, Son and Holy Spirit together

"I appeal to you, brethren, by Our Lord Jesus Christ and by the love of the Spirit, to strive together with me in your prayer to God (the Father) on my behalf" (Romans 15:30).

"Through Him (Christ) we both have access in one Spirit to the Father" (Ephesians 2:18).

"pray in the Holy Spirit; keep yourselves in the love of God (the Father); wait for the mercy of Our Lord Jesus Christ unto eternal life" (Jude 20-21).

Father, Son and Holy Spirit are the One Divine Reality which we, Christians, believe in when we speak about the Blessed Trinity.

We firmly believe that there is only One God. Basing ourselves on the revelation of Jesus Christ and the teaching of Sacred Scripture, we believe that in that one God, there is Father, Son and Holy Spirit. Human words fail us here, but what else can we expect when we speak about the overwhelming Reality in God?

4.3 'The Father is greater than I'

Watchtower argument

At the Last Supper Jesus said: "If you loved me you would have been glad to hear that I was going to the Father, for the Father is greater than I am" *(John 14:28)*. If the Father is greater than Jesus, it means that Jesus is not God.

Response

Jesus does not mean that the Father is greater from the point of view of divinity. But, within the Blessed Trinity, the Father is the Person on whom the Son as Son totally depends. Whenever Jesus speaks about the Father, he always stresses both aspects.

(a) that the Son receives everything from the Father;

(b) that the Son receives **everything** *(the whole divinity)* from him.

Read once more the text which we analysed in chapter two, no 2.1.2. The Son receives from the Father *(a)* divine knowledge; *(b)* giving life; *(c)* being judge; *(d)* deserving of divine worship. These things belong intrinsically to God. God could not give these things to someone outside the Godhead. They express the divine nature itself.

The Father, one Person in God, precisely is 'Father' because he passes on the whole divine nature to the 'Son', who is the Second Person in God. In other words: Father and Son possess and share the same nature, but the Father as Father gives; the Son as Son receives. The Father lives totally in giving all to the Son; the Son lives totally in receiving all from the Father.

This is, therefore what Jesus means by the statement quoted above. "If you loved me you would have been glad to hear that I was going to the Father." If you realise how I, as "Son" in the Trinity, live completely by my dependence on the Father - my loving 'receiving' from him, you would have been glad. For the Father is greater than I: I depend totally on him as my Father."

In the same chapter *(John 14,7-14)* Jesus had just explained this intimate relationship with the Father:

"If you knew me you would know my Father too"
(John 14:7)
(means: *If you realise that I am the Second Person in God, that I am the Son who have everything I have from the Father, you would know him too*).

"Anyone who has seen me has seen the Father" (John 14:9).
(means: *I myself am the revelation of God. Knowing (seeing) me as the Son, necessarily implies knowing the Father who gave all to me*) .

4.4 The Holy Spirit

Watch tower argument

You speak of the Holy Spirit as a new person in God.
However, in the New Testament, like in the Old, the Spirit or
the Holy Spirit is nothing else than God's power. One reason
for your interpretation is a bias in your translations by which
you see the Holy Spirit where the original has a different
reading.
In Hebrews 9:14, for instance Christians translate
"the eternal Spirit". However, the original just says:
"an everlasting spirit" (NWT).

Response

There are a number of passages in which the word 'Spirit' could
indeed be translated more vaguely as God's 'Spirit' in a general
sense. Many standard translations do so. But in other instances
it is clear that there the Spirit points to the new Person in God
revealed by Jesus.

The New World Translation used by Jehovah's Witnesses
deliberately attempts to erase those references in the New
Testament to the Holy Spirit as a separate reality in God. This
effort to expunge New Testament teaching on the Holy Spirit
runs parallel to the NWT's attempt to erase the Scriptures'
teaching about Jesus' divinity (see chapter 3!).

The following should be noted:

• In Hebrews 9:14 there is no definite article before "eternal
spirit" in the Greek text. However, the expression "Holy
Spirit" and its parallels in New Testament usage occurs both
with the article or without, while clearly meaning "the Holy

Spirit". For its usage without article see, for instance:
Hebrews 2:4; 6:4; Acts 1:2; 6:5; 7:54; 8:15; 9:17; 2 Timothy
1:14. Incidentally, this is the same as for the word "God".
At times it has the article, at times not. In Hebrews 9:14 the
expression definitely means "*the* eternal Spirit".

• In 1 Timothy 4:1, where we read: "the Spirit says", the
NWT substitutes "the Spirit" with "the inspired utterance".
However, the Holy Spirit does speak to people as we see in
parallel texts such as Acts 8:29; 10:19; 11:12; 13:2; etc.
Why tamper with God's Word?

• The same applies to other attempts to minimise mention
of the Holy Spirit, such as using of the Spirit the pronoun
"it" (John 14:17), or writing "spirit", without capitals
(as in Romans 8,23; 1 Peter 3:18-19; etc.).

4.5 Father, Son and Spirit in one verse

Watchtower argument

Christians often adduce the texts you quote above (in no
4.2.1 to 4.2.5). The fact that Father, Son and Spirit are
mentioned in one verse does not prove that they are three
Persons in God. Scripture also mentions Abraham, Isaac and
Jacob in one verse; or John, James, and Peter. Does that
make them new Trinities?

Response

The mention of Father, Son and Holy Spirit together in one verse does not by itself show that they are three Realities in God. However, in the passages quoted above the context should be carefully noted.

Abraham, Isaac and Jacob are mentioned together because they were three patriarchs. Peter, John and James were three important Apostles, perhaps a core team within the group since they accompany Jesus on a number of important occasions (Mark 5:37; 9:2; 13:3; 14:33-37). The fact that such people are mentioned together so often does establish them as some form of 'trinity', though not a divine trinity of course!

With regards to Father, Son and Holy Spirit the grouping happens *within the context of their divine life and activity.* Father, Son and Holy Spirit together liberate us from sin, make us adopted children, fill our lives with their presence and help us on our journey. It is this specific togetherness in divine activity that reveals them to us as three Realities within the same God.

4.6 The word 'Trinity'

Watchtower argument

The word " Trinity" never occurs in Sacred Scripture, neither is it found amongst the early Christian writers. In fact, the terms used by Christians to express their belief in the Trinity are only of a later date, certainly not earlier than the fourth century after Christ.

This teaching *can*, therefore, not belong to the inspired message of Scripture or be an essential part of Christian doctrine.

Response

We have to carefully distinguish between the substance that is being believed in and the words used to express it. The fact that Christians keep reflecting on the substance of their faith, and use new words in order to express that substance, does not mean that they have changed it.

Take an everyday example. While visiting a tribal area in Kenya, I may read in a guide that the tribe in question forms an egalitarian society, lives from a hand-to-mouth economy and follows matriarchal rules of inheritance. The tribal people in question may never have heard These words. But when I talk to them, they will confirm the substance of it by what they say. This is what happens with regard to matters of doctrine.

Consider our belief in God. To describe God today we use words such as infinite, omniscient, transcendent, immanent (he is present in the whole universe), and so on. Such terms by themselves are not found in Scripture, but they do express truths that are found in it, though the substance is expressed in a different way.

The same applies to the doctrine of the Holy Trinity. The substance of Jesus' revealing to us that God is Father, Son and Spirit is undeniable as I have shown above. In the course of time Christians needed to express this more clearly, especially when heresies arose that denied one or other aspect of the reality they believed in.

It is to define the true meaning of our Christian faith and the message of Scripture against the misunderstandings propounded by heretics that Church Councils in the third and fourth centuries worked out the trinitarian terminology that we use today. This terminology, being human, is of necessity imperfect.

At the same time it is also helpful, because it makes us see things much more clearly.

4.6 Three 'Persons' in the Blessed Trinity

Watchtower argument

Christians say that there are three *Persons* in God: Father, Son and Holy Spirit. They profess at the same time that there is only one God. But These two statements are completely contradictory.

To be a true "person", Father, Son, and Holy Spirit must be able to act independently. Each person has his own mind and takes his own decisions. But this means that there are really three Gods. The old trinitarian gods of the pagan world have thus been reintroduced into Christianity in a new guise.

Response

The objection would be valid if the word "Person" used in the trinitarian formula were to have the same meaning as the word "person" has in modern English. But such is not the case.

The use of the term "Person" in the Trinity was introduced by the Greek Fathers of the Church as an equivalent to *hypostasis*, subsistence. What they were trying to express is that somehow, though God is One, God is not solitary. Within the One God there are mutual relationships, as it were different faces that reflect one another.

In human language this is sometimes expressed as the Father reflecting on himself and thus giving birth to the Son, and

Father and Son reflecting on their mutual love which becomes the Holy Spirit. Since we are talking about God's deepest essence, we are dealing with first-class mystery, and human terms will always remain inadequate.

Using the term "Person" is not a fortunate turn of phrase when we speak of the Trinity today. For in present-day usage, a "person" refers to an individual who can independently think, decide and act. This is not how it is in the Trinity. The early Church Councils clearly expressed that Father, Son and Holy Spirit are One God. They have one intelligence, one will, and one combined external action, if we may use such human terms about God.

Father, Son and Spirit possess one divine nature and are not distinct in anything else except their mutual relationship to each other.

Christian belief in the Trinity emphasises the conviction that God is *personal*. In God's self-revelation to us in the incarnation of the Son and the continued presence of the Spirit, we experience a glimpse of the enormous depths of relationships and love in God. In however small a way, we share in the richness of these relationships in God by our awareness of Father, Son and Holy Spirit in God.

Conclusion

If we may sum up the meaning of our Christian belief in the Trinity in non-theological terms, it comes to this. God, cosmic Mind and uncreated Love, is so intensely personal that we experience God as caring Parent, intimate Brother and inner Spark in us, all at the same time. The personal dimensions in God are inexhaustible.

5. LIFE AFTER DEATH

What does the Watchtower Society teach?

The Watchtower Society insists that there is no life after death for ordinary human beings. Belief in the immortality of the soul is a device of the devil, they say. For them, death is final, ultimate; and the greatest punishment for trespasses is annihilation. After death, a person will not feel, understand, or suffer. There is, consequently, no hell.

To the question: "Will there be any resurrection?", the standard answer states that: "There will be resurrection but God distinguishes two classes."

A small group of 144,000 elect will rise to life and will reign with Christ in heaven. This resurrection will affect only the faithful servants of God Jehovah. This will include a privileged core among the Jehovah's Witnesses, their ancestors and their scripture scholars.

For others who have tried to serve Jehovah or good people who during their lifetime never met or heard of Jehovah's Witnesses, there will be a probation time in the millennium, a testing of faithfulness to God Jehovah. They are the 'Jonadab class' (Jeremiah 35:1-19). If, during the period of trial, they prove their loyalty to God Jehovah, they will be in some kind of paradise on earth, the 'new world'. They will live in this earthly paradise for ever, but they will not go to heaven. And, if they do not pass the test, they will have to die again, and for ever.

5.1 What does Scripture say?

"All of us must appear before the judgment seat of Christ, so that each may receive recompense for what has been done in the body, whether good or evil" (2 Corinthians 5:10).

The teaching of Jesus Christ commands us not to fear a testing in the millennium, but to be afraid of God's judgment, which begins at the time of death.

"In flaming fire, inflicting vengeance on those who do not know God and on those who do not obey the gospel of Our Lord Jesus. These will suffer the punishment of eternal destruction, separated from the presence of the Lord and from the glory of his might" (2 Thessalonians 1:8-9).

"For to me, living is Christ and dying is gain. If I am to live in the flesh, that means fruitful labour for me; and I do not know which I prefer. I am hard pressed between the two; my desire is to depart and to be with Christ, for that is far better; but to remain in the flesh is more necessary for you" (Philippians 1:21-24).

Hence, we have God who will judge us. From him we will receive the reward of eternal life, or we may be thrown into hell to be separated from God for ever.

"Do not fear those who kill the body but cannot kill the soul; rather fear him who can destroy both soul and body in hell" (Matthew 10:28).

5.2 'Hell' in the New Testament

Watchtower argument

When Christ says: "Do not fear those who kill the body but cannot kill the soul; rather fear him who can destroy both soul and body in hell" (Matthew 10:28), he means: "Do not fear those who kill the body but cannot kill the soul; rather fear him who can bury soul and body in a grave".

Response

The word used for 'hell' in the Greek text is *gehenna*, a burning rubbish dump outside Jerusalem which at the time of Christ became an image of the place of eternal punishment. In Christ's mouth is refers to the real 'hell' of God's everlasting punishment (see Matthew 5:22; 5:29-30; 18:9; 23:33; Mark 9:43, 45-47).

If we could accept the Watchtower interpretation that hell is a grave, the result of the above verse would suggest that Christ commands us to be afraid of those who after our death, will bury our dead body in a grave. Thus, this implies that the burial of our dead bodies is more terrible and much worse than death by killing. No logical thinking person could accept such a teaching that hell is a grave. Why should a corpse be afraid to be buried in a grave?

Listen again to Jesus in the parallel text of Luke's gospel:

"I tell you my friends, do not fear those who kill the body, and after that can do nothing more. But I will warn you whom to fear; fear him who, after he has killed, has authority to cast into hell. Yes, I tell you, fear him! (Luke 12:4-5).

These above verses declare very strongly and clearly of whom we should be afraid. If hell means the grave, then we should believe that Christ as a human being in Gethsemane was not afraid of his assassins who would be tormenting and crucifying him, but was afraid of Nicodemus and Joseph of Arimathea who buried Christ's body in a grave (John 19:38-42). Scripture recognises the difference between hell and a grave!

5.3 Christ's descent into hell

Watchtower argument

You traditional Christians are contradicting yourselves since in your 'professional faith' you say: "We believe in one God... he was crucified, died and was buried. He entered into hell and on the third day he rose again". So he died and stepped into hell, which means: he went into the grave. Thus you yourselves are saying that 'hell' is 'grave'.

Response

In some old English texts, the word 'hell' was also used for the 'realm of the dead' (*she'ol* in Hebrew; *hades* in Greek). This referred to a place underneath the earth where the souls of the dead were believed to remain until judgment day. See Matthew 11:23; Luke 16:23; Revelation 20:13-14. This is the meaning of the word in the ancient Creed.

After death, Jesus Christ was buried. This means that the body was placed into a grave. However, his soul did not die but when it left the body of Christ at the time of bodily death, the soul of Jesus went to preach to the 'imprisoned spirits' (1 Peter 3:18-19) who were the souls in Hades (the place of the dead) waiting for the Messiah to free them.

This, however, is distinct from hell properly speaking which is the place reserved for the damned.

When Christ died, his human soul was immediately embraced by the Father. That is why he tells the Good Thief crucified at his side: "Truly I tell you, today you will be with me in paradise" (Luke 23:43).

5.4 'Today you will be in paradise'

Watchtower argument

The comma is put in the wrong place. This verse should read, "Truly I am telling you today, you will be with me in paradise". In other words, truly I am telling you today - you will be with me in paradise (that is: after two thousand years in the 'New World')."

Response

Many times during his teaching Christ addressed the people with these words, "Truly, truly, I am telling you!" (Matthew 26:21; John 6:47; etc.). Not once did he say: "Truly, truly *today* I tell you". In this case Jesus spoke the word "today" as he was hanging on the cross, just before he died. This does not mean "Today I tell you". Christ clearly said to the thief, "Today you will be with me in paradise".

5.5 The meaning of 'paradise'

Watchtower argument

How could the thief be with Christ in paradise on the same day or even in heaven - as traditional Christians call, since Christ did not ascend to heaven until forty days after his resurrection? (Acts 1:3; 1:9-11)

Response

Paradise is the union of the soul with God after death. After he died, the soul of the thief was free of his flesh and was united with Christ, God. And the soul fully participated in the happiness which people on earth call paradise. After death the soul unites with God at once. The Apostle Paul also refers to this subject in the letter to the Philippians:

> "For to me, living is Christ and dying is gain. If I am to live in the flesh, that means fruitful labour for me; and I do not know which to prefer. I am hard pressed between the two: my desire is to depart and be with Christ, for that is far better. But to remain in the flesh is more necessary for you" (Philippians 1:21-24).

Scripture promises eternal reward in heaven to all who have lived good lives on earth.

> "In my Father's house there are many dwelling places. If it were not so, would I have told you that I go to prepare a place for you?" (John 14:2).

> "Rejoice and be glad, for your reward is great in heaven, for in the same way they persecuted the prophets who were before you" (Matthew 5:12).

> "For we know that if the earthly tent we live in is destroyed, we have a building from God, a house not made with hands, eternal in the heavens" (2 Corinthians 5:1).

> "Because of the hope laid up for you in heaven. You have heard of this hope before in the word of the truth, the Gospel" (Colossians 1:5).

5.6 No two classes at the Resurrection

Watchtower argument

There will be life in heaven but with one big difference: it will be reserved for a small group of the chosen ones, only one-hundred-forty-four thousand (Revelation 14:1).

A second group, forming a large crowd, will be chosen by
God Jehovah after Armageddon, the final battle. They also
will live for eternity but not in heaven. They will stay on
earth. They will be an earthly chosen race for the "New
World" ("Then I saw a new heaven and a new earth"
Revelation 21:1).

Response

Revelation 14:1 should not be taken literally. All prophecies
written in the book of Revelations are illustrated with
numbers that have a *symbolical meaning*. Probably the
144,000 stands for twelve times twelve times one thousand:
the twelve tribes of Israel (Revelation 7:4-8). The number
twelve symbolises completeness. In the Old Testament God
chose the twelve tribes to inhabit the land of Israel, and in the
New Testament Jesus chose the twelve apostles to initiate the
kingdom of God on earth.

The last number, the "one thousand", represents all the
people who have followed God's teachings and placed God
first in their lives from the guidance of the law and the
apostles. If John had given a literal number of people in the
book of Revelation it would have been a much more accurate,
specific total.

Will there only be 144,000 people in heaven?

Jehovah's Witnesses rely on this literal interpretation of the
number (Revelation 7:3-8; 14:1). However Revelation further
declares that besides the one-hundred-and forty-four thousand,
there were *the elders*.

*"And they sing a new song before the throne and before the
four living creatures and before the elders. No one could*

learn that song except the one hundred forty-four thousand
who have been redeemed from the earth" (Revelation 14:3).

Revelation 4:10 declares: "The twenty four elders fell down
and worshipped" (Revelation 5:14). Plus in Revelation 5:13, we
find all the living beings in creation in heaven, on the earth, and
under the earth worshipping God. Hence, it is evident that with
the Lamb were one-hundred-forty-four thousand plus twenty-
four elders, plus a countless number of people.

"After this I looked, and there was a great multitude that no
one could count, from every nation, from all tribes and
peoples and languages, standing before the throne and
before the Lamb, robed in white, with palm branches in their
hands. They cried out in a loud voice, saying, 'salvation
belongs to our God who is seated on the throne, and to the
Lamb!' And all the angels stood around the throne, around
the elders and the four living creatures, and they fell on their
faces before the throne and worshipped God"
(Revelation 7:9-11).

Now we can perceive that besides the 144,000 and the 24
elders, there were a great multitude, a number no one was able
to count from different nations, tribes and generations.
Revelation clearly declares the multitude was **in heaven**, in the
same place where the 144,000 and 24 elders were before the
throne and before the countenance of the Lamb where they sang
their hymns.

According to Watchtower doctrine, the great multitude will
not live in heaven but in the "new world", on earth. However,
the book of Revelation does not differentiate between the place
where the countless multitude will be and the place where the
144,000 and the twenty-four-elders will be.

5.7 The 'other sheep'

Watchtower argument

There are two chosen classes: a heavenly class and the earthly class of "the New World" on earth. Jesus taught this when he said: "I have other sheep that do not belong to this fold" (John 10:16). Jesus' own sheep are the Jehovah's Witnesses who go to heaven. The others will remain on earth in a New World.

Response

Read the whole verse:

"I have other sheep that do not belong to this fold. I must bring them also, and they will listen to my voice. So there will be one flock, one shepherd" (John 10:16).

This verse contains two sentences. From the whole verse we can conclude:"There will be **one flock and one shepherd**". Hence, all who listen and obey will be chosen in the same class or flock.

Why quote only the first half of the verse, or maintain that the "other sheep" belong to "new world"? Any intelligent, independent, freeminded person without prejudice can at once observe dishonesty in Watchtower argumentation.

5.8 Those who 'inherit the earth'

Watchtower argument

Read what Jesus says: "Blessed are the poor in spirit, for theirs is the kingdom of heaven. Blessed are the meek, for they will inherit the earth" (Matthew 5:3-4). In those two verses Jesus differentiates between two classes. The first class, "the poor fold", will receive the kingdom of heaven. However, the second class will possess the earth.

Response

To prove the absurdity of such an interpretation, here is the full report of Jesus' teaching, of all his beatitudes from which Jehovah's Witnesses extract only two and change them into classes:

"Blessed are the poor in spirit, for theirs is the kingdom of heaven.
Blessed are those who mourn, for they will be comforted.
Blessed are the meek, for they will inherit the earth.
Blessed are those who hunger and thirst for righteousness, for they will be filled.
Blessed are the merciful, for they will receive mercy.
Blessed are the poor in heart, for they will see God.
Blessed are the peace makers, for they will be called the children of God.
Blessed are those who are persecuted for righteousness' sake, for theirs is the kingdom of heaven.
Blessed are you when people revile you and persecute you and utter all kinds of evil against you falsely on my account. Rejoice and be glad, for your reward is great in heaven, for in the same way they persecuted the prophets who were before you" (Matthew 5:2-12).

If beatitude one and three indicate two distinct classes whom God will separate in afterlife, what about the other seven groups ? Does God distinguish *nine* classes?

If we distort the Word of God we can make it say anything that suits our self-made doctrines. The sad truth is that the doctrine of the 'two classes' was invented as a face saving exercise by the leaders of the Watchtower Society (see chapter 7, no 7.1.2).

5.9 'The person who sins shall die'

Watchtower argument

Sinners do not go to judgment. They are annihilated at death. In the same way our body dies, so also our soul dies. Read this verse from the Old Testament: "The person who sins shall die" (Ezekiel 18:20).

Response

How is it possible to base a theory on a fragment of a verse? In the next verse and seven verses further in the same chapter, we are told which death is being referred to. We observe that for Jehovah's Witnesses only a fragment of a verse is always enough to declare their teachings as if it were the whole Scripture proclamation.

We should read the whole text:

"If the wicked however, renounces all the sins he has committed, respects my laws and is law abiding and upright, he will most certainly live; he will not die" (Ezekiel 18:27).

"Again, when the wicked turn away from the wickedness they have committed and do what is lawful and right, they shall save their life" (Ezekiel 18:27).

Do life and death in these verses not rather refer to spiritual life and death?

Notice that Ezekiel 18:20 literally says: *"The soul* who sins will die". Though the sinner may well be punished by physical death on earth, the worst is that he or she dies a spiritual death. Such a death does not involve annihilation, but eternal punishment by God.

In the New Testament we have similar expressions:

"But the widow who lives for pleasure is dead even while she lives (1 Timothy 5:6).

"And when you were dead in trespasses and the uncircumcision of your flesh, God made you alive together with him, when he forgave us all our trespasses" (Colossians 2:13).

"You were dead through the trespasses and sins in which you once lived, following the course of this world, following the ruler of the power of the air, the spirit that is now at work among those who are disobedient" (Ephesians 2:1-2).

5.10 The fate of the human soul

Watchtower argument

The immortality of the soul is an illusion.

There is no difference between beasts and human beings as Scripture teaches:

"For the fate of humans and the fate of animals is the same; as one dies, so dies the other. They all have the same breath, and humans have no advantage over the animals; for all is vanity. All go to one place; all are from the dust, and all turn to dust again. Who knows whether the human spirit goes upward and the spirit of animals goes downwards to the earth?" (Ecclesiastes 3:19-21).

Response

If we were to base all of Gods' words on only one passage, as Jehovah's Witnesses often do, we would remain with questions here. Still, in these verses there is the acknowledgment of the human spirit (Ecclesiastes 3:21). Remember, this spirit is the soul which God gives us as part of creation (Genesis 2:7).

Ecclesiastes honestly cannot say whether it goes upwards or downwards at death, but he is not claiming that it does <u>not</u> go upwards as the Jehovah's Witnesses do.

In addition, we draw the reader's attention to the last verses of the book:

"For God will call our deeds to judgment, all that was hidden, be it good or bad" (Ecclesiastes 12:14).

"The dust returns to the earth from which it came and the spirit returns to God who gave it" (Ecclesiastes 12:7).

So by the end of the book the author answers the question he utters in chapter 3.

If we only read part of Scripture, we can question even the existence of God for there is another verse in Scripture which says: "The fool says in his heart: 'there is no God'." (Psalm 14:1)

If we discard the beginning of the sentence above, "The fool says in his heart", we will be left with the remaining sentence, "There is no God".

This example shows the Watchtower method of dealing with Scripture: "A human being is nothing more than a beast" (Ecclesiastes 3:19). They ignore the context of the passage which reveals in verse 18 that it is a fool who speaks thus. There are many other verses with similar contents in the book of Ecclesiastes: "Let us eat, drink, enjoy every possible pleasure"; but each time he begins by saying: "I said to myself".

"I said to myself, 'come now, I will make a test of pleasure; enjoy yourself'. But again, this also was vanity" (Ecclesiastes 2:1).

He did not teach under inspiration that this is the best attitude to life; he only had such thoughts in his heart. Like a foolish person who says: "There is no God". But remember that this same author towards the end of his book declares:

"And the dust returns to the earth as it was, and the breath returns to God who gave it" (Ecclesiastes 12:7).

Conclusion

After death all people face God's judgment. Those who have sinned will be punished. Those who have acted well, will be rewarded by God in heaven.

There are no two classes among the saved. All the saved will share God's love and joy in heaven.

6. CHRISTIAN LIFE

6.1 Birthdays

Watchtower argument

The only two birthday celebrations spoken of in the Bible were held by persons who did not worship Jehovah (Genesis 40:20-22; Mark 6:21, 22, 24-27) The early Christians did not celebrate birthdays. The custom of celebrating birthdays comes from ancient false religions. True Christians give gifts and have good times together at other times during the year.

Response

Scripture tells us that life is a gift from God. The day of birth is a happy event for both mother and father. Job expressed his deep sorrow by lamenting the event most important in a human life: the day of his birth (Job 3:1-26). Devout people, however, would thank God the gift of life. The whole of Psalm 139 is a prayer of thanksgiving people may well have recited on their birth day.

"Thou didst form my inward parts. Thou didst knit me together in my mother's womb. I praise thee, for thou art wonderful" (Psalm 139:13-14).

The Hellenists at the time of Christ loved birthday parties and at times excesses happened such as at Herod's feast (Mark 6:21-29). The early Christians objected to the pagan excesses, but they did not object to thanking God, and one's parents and family, for the gift of life. There is no reason why Christians should not celebrate birthdays in this spirit.

6. 2 Christmas

Watchtower argument

Jesus was not born on December 25. He was born about October 1, a time of year when shepherds kept their flocks out-of-doors at night (Luke 2:8-12). Jesus never commanded Christians to celebrate his birth. Rather, he told his disciples to memorialise, or remember, his death. (Luke 22:19, 20) Christmas and its customs come from ancient false religions.

Response

The feast of Christmas incorporates some European cultural customs that predate Christianity. Such customs include the use of holly and mistletoe and the Christmas tree: evergreens which are signs of life in the middle of winter. They were originally used in a pagan religious context, but their meaning was transformed by their incorporation in a Christian feast.

There are many examples of this in salvation history. Circumcision was a pagan custom long before God enjoined it on Abraham with a new meaning (Genesis 17:9-14). Baptism was a Hellenistic and a Jewish rite. Jesus adopted it and transformed it to express Christian salvation (John 3:5; Matthew 28:19).

The feast of Christmas itself is of Christian origin. The Incarnation, the Word becoming flesh in Jesus (John 1:14), was the beginning of our salvation. It is natural for Christians to celebrate this day. The precise date of the feast is immaterial. It is the celebration of the salvific event that matters.

In Scripture, God the Father himself honours Jesus' birthday. At birth a new born child was put on the father's knees (Genesis 30:3; 50:23). The father would then give it a name (Hosea 1:3-9) and thus acknowledge the child as his own. This is what God the Father said to Jesus:

"You are my Son. Today I have begotten you" (Psalm 2:7).

"He has become as much superior to the angels as the name he has obtained is more excellent than theirs. For to what angel did God ever say: 'Thou art my Son, today I have begotten thee'?" (Hebrews 1:4-5; see also Acts 13:33).

Christians have celebrated the feast of Christ's birth from very early times, but the date has changed in the course of time. The feast was originally called Epiphany, 'Appearance', after Titus 2:11: "The grace of God has appeared for the salvation of all people". The Orthodox Churches still celebrate Epiphany as their Christmas.

In Western Europe Christmas, as Christ's birthday, was separated from Epiphany, the feast of Christ's 'manifesting himself to the world' in his meeting with the three wise men from the East (Matthew 2:1-12). The date was deliberately fixed on the 25th of December to make it replace the pagan custom of celebrating the winter solstice (the return of the sun). For Jesus Christ, not any pagan sun god, deserved to be celebrated. Christmas is therefore not of pagan origin; just the opposite. It superseded the pagan religion.

6.3 Easter

Watchtower argument

Christians are mistaken in thinking that Jesus rose with his body. This is not the case. After his death Jesus rose again as a spirit. Jehovah disintegrated Jesus' body into invisible atomic particles during the three days of entombment. Christ never told his followers to celebrate his resurrection. He wanted them to commemorate his death. Easter, therefore, is misplaced. Easter customs, such as the use of eggs and rabbits, derive from paganism. The early Christians did not celebrate Easter, nor do true Christians today.

Response

All New Testament books witness to Jesus' Resurrection. They clearly proclaim that he rose with his body.

"See my hands and my feet, that it is I myself; handle me, and see; for a spirit has not flesh and bones as you see that I have" (Luke 24:39).

Not only did the Apostles touch Jesus' wounds (Luke 24:40; John 20:27). He ate and drank with them (Luke 24:41-43; Acts 10:41). They witnessed to the fact that Jesus' flesh experienced no corruption (Acts 2:31; 13:37). Without belief in the bodily resurrection of Christ, they tell us, our faith is in vain (1 Corinthians 15:12-19). Read Paul's explanation about the risen body in 1 Corinthians 15:35-50.

Christians, therefore, have always celebrated Easter, as much as they have remembered Christ during Holy Week. When Jesus Christ, at the last supper, said: "Do this in remembrance of me" (Luke 22:19), he did not refer only to his death, but also to his resurrection. Yes, 'we proclaim the Lord's death until he comes' (1 Corinthians 11:26), but it was a death only meaningful through his resurrection: "if Christ has not been raised, our preaching is in vain" (1 Corinthians 15:14).

"The Lord Jesus who was put to death for our trespasses and raised for our justification" (Romans 4:25).

"But if we have died with Christ, we believe we shall also live with him. For we know that Christ being raised from the dead will never die again; death no longer has dominion over him" (Romans 6:8-9).

Every Sunday is a celebration of Easter. Christians moved their weekly worship from the Saturday (*the Sabbath*) to the Sunday precisely because Christ rose on the Sunday, "the first day of the week" (Matthew 28:1; Mark 16:2; Luke 24:2; John 20:1). That is when they came together to celebrate the Eucharist (Acts 20:7; 1 Corinthians 16:2). They called it "the Lord's day": the day when Christ had been definitely shown to be Lord and God.

"We no longer celebrate the Sabbath but live under observance of the Lord's day, on which day also our life is arisen...." **Ignatius of Antioch, 110 AD**

"Christians have the custom of coming together on a fixed day before dawn and of singing a song to Christ honouring him as God..." **Pliny the Younger, 113 AD**

"We keep the meeting of our community on a Sunday because it is the first day of the week... because Jesus Christ, our Saviour, rose on this day." **Justin the Martyr, 150 AD**

6.4 The communion of saints

Watchtower argument

The dead cannot do anything or feel anything. We cannot help them, and they cannot hurt us (Psalm 146:4; Ecclesiastes 9:5, 10). The soul dies; it does not live on after death (Ezekiel 18:4). But sometimes wicked angels, called demons, pretend to be the spirits of the dead. Any customs that have to do with fear of or worship of the dead are wrong (Isaiah 8:19). There is no reason to worship the dead or to fear them. The veneration of the saints is wrong.

Response

The Christian belief in the communion of saints rests on the Scriptural teaching that in Christ we have become one large body of believers. We belong together.

"As in one body we have many members, and all the members do not have the same function, so we, though many, are one body in Christ and individually members of each other" (Romans 12:4-5; see also 1 Corinthians 12:12-26).

All Christians are called 'saints' in the New Testament and this applies also to those who have died (Matthew 27,52). Those who are still alive and those who have 'fallen asleep' will be raised together on the last day (1 Thessalonians 4:14-17; 1 Corinthians 15:51-52). Some of the 'saints' are still struggling on earth (Revelation 5:8; 13:7, 10) while others are already with the Lamb in heaven (Revelation 19:8; 7:9-17).

It is natural for Christians to honour the saints who have preceded them. It is also natural that they offer prayers for those who have died.

"Judas took up a collection, man by man, to the amount of two thousand drachmas of silver, and sent it to Jerusalem to provide for a sin offering. In doing this he acted very well and honourably, taking account of the resurrection. For if he were not expecting that those who had fallen would rise again, it would have been superfluous and foolish to pray for the dead. But if he was looking forward to the splendid reward that is laid up for those who fall asleep in godliness, it was a holy and pious thought. Therefore he made atonement for the dead, that they might be delivered from their sin" (2 Maccabees 12:43-45).

"Otherwise, what do people mean by being baptised on behalf of the dead? If the dead are not raised at all, why are people baptised on their behalf?" (1 Corinthians 15:29).

6.5 Jesus' Cross

Watchtower argument

Jesus did not die on a cross. He died on a pole, or a stake. The Greek word translated by "cross" in many Bibles meant just one piece of timber. The symbol of the cross comes from ancient false religions. The cross was not used or worshipped by the early Christians. Therefore, do you think it would be right to use a cross in worship? Read Deuteronomy 7:26; 1 Corinthians 10:14.

Response

The Romans were accustomed to executing criminals on a high pole with a cross beam. The cross consisted of two beams nailed together in a cruciform fashion. The person condemned to death was, at times, just required to carry the cross beam. At the place of execution the two beams were attached together.

Whatever the shape of Jesus' cross, because he died for us on this instrument of torture (Galatians 3:13; 5:11), the cross is held out to us by Scripture as the symbol of his redemptive death.

"Lest the cross of Christ be emptied of its power. For the word of the cross is folly to those who are perishing" (1 Corinthians 1:17-18).

"God cancelled the bond which stood against us with its legal demands; this he set aside, nailing it to the cross" (Colossians 2:14).

"Far be it from me to glory except in the cross of Christ, by which the world has been crucified to me, and I to the world" (Galatians 6:14).

It is extremely fitting, therefore, that we use images of the cross in our Christian worship.

6.6 Blood Transfusion

Watchtower argument

It is forbidden to take blood under any circumstances (see Genesis 9:3; Leviticus 17:14 and Acts 15:28-29). The Creator has laid an absolute ban on taking in blood to sustain life: "You must not eat the blood; pour it out on the ground like water. Do not eat it, so that it may go well with you and your children after you, because you will be doing what is right" (Deuteronomy 12:23-25; 15:23; Leviticus 7:26-27; Ezekiel 33:25).

For this reason blood transfusion is forbidden by God. We may not ignore God's law on blood even in an emergency. We should rather die than receive blood.

Response

The Scriptural texts quoted do not forbid the taking of blood under any circumstances. What they forbid is consuming *(eating)* blood. Because blood was considered to be sacred, and was used in sacrifices to express the gift of life (both from God and returned to God through the sacrifice), it was considered wrong to eat blood. That is why Jews even today do not eat the meat of any animal if the blood is not first drained from the animal after slaughter.

With regard to blood transfusion, it is wrong to misinterpret the meaning of Scripture, and apply its message to a new situation in our time which was not intended by the inspired authors of the Old and New Testaments.

Also remember:

- Saving a human life is a priority. For this, laws at times can and must be broken. Jesus himself taught this principle when the Pharisees wanted to prevent him from curing a sick person on the Sabbath because it broke the law of the Sabbath rest (Matthew 12:9-13; Mark 3:1-5; Luke 6:6-10; 13:10-17; 14:1-6; John 5:1-16).

- God does not allow us to take our own life. Does the refusal to accept blood transfusion not amount to a degree of suicide?

•When a person receives a blood transfusion, he or she does not eat someone else's blood. Rather, he or she shares somehow in the gift of life of the other person. Since blood transfusion in this way helps us to share life and extend life and save life, it is just the kind of thing which God expects us to do if we are to take seriously both the Old Testament commandments of protecting life and the New Testament principle of love for our neighbour.

7. THE WATCHTOWER SOCIETY

The official name of the organisation that holds Jehovah's Witnesses together is the Watch Tower Bible and Tract Society. Overall authority rests with the Governing Body, located at the world headquarters in Brooklyn. It consists of 12 members.

The organisation exercises tight control over the membership:

• The use of the organisation's own Scripture translation, the New World Translation, is obligatory on all.

• The Governing Body publishes binding guidelines on doctrine and practice in its regular bi-monthly magazines 'The Watch Tower' and 'Awake!'. 'The Watch Tower' comes out in 128 languages, and 'Awake!' in 81 languages, each with a circulation of more than 10,000,000 copies. Books, booklets, and tracts are being distributed by the hundreds of millions. The contents are strictly controlled by the Governing Body at the world headquarters in Brooklyn, New York.

• The Governing Body sends representatives each year to 15 or more "zones" worldwide to confer with the branch representatives in each zone. In the branch offices, there are Branch Committees of from three to seven members to oversee the work in the lands under their jurisdiction. Many of the branches have facilities for printing, some operating high-speed rotary presses. The country or area served by each branch is divided into districts, and the districts, in turn, are divided into circuits. Each circuit has in it about 20 congregations. A district overseer visits the circuits in his district in rotation. Two assemblies are held annually for each circuit. There is also a circuit overseer, and he visits each congregation in his circuit usually twice a year, assisting the Witnesses in organising and doing the preaching work in the territory assigned to that congregation.

• Annual reports have to be sent in from all congregations, circuits, districts and branches to headquarters in Brooklyn. Any form of dissent is immediately labeled 'apostasy'. Dissenting members are banned through 'disfellowshipping'.

Through its actions, the Governing Body has proved to be a group of untrustworthy and misguided spiritual leaders. I say this for three reasons:

• They deprive the members of the true message of God's Word.

• They proclaim prophecies and teachings they know to be untrue.

• They usurp a spiritual authority that is not theirs.

7.1 The Watchtower Society deprives its members of the true message of God's Word

7.1.1 The New World Translation

The NWT is a version of Sacred Scripture in which key passages have been deliberately manipulated in order to boost Jehovah's Witness doctrine. See chapter 3 about this.

By imposing this translation on the members and forbidding the use of other Bible translations, the members are effectively barred from hearing the genuine Word of God.

> *"Woe to you, hypocrites! Because you shut the kingdom of heaven against men; for you neither enter yourselves, nor allow those who would enter to go in" (Matthew 23:14).*

7.1.2 Interpretation of Scripture

While it is claimed that doctrine is based on Scripture, it is the interpretation published in Watch Tower that is imposed as binding. Members may not hold, or openly discuss with other Jehovah's Witnesses, opinions that differ from orthodox Watch Tower doctrine.

Terrible doctrines are invented out of thin air, as a face saving exercise for the blind spiritual guides in Brooklyn.

One such example is the doctrine of the two classes: the 144,000 'elect' and the 'Jonadab class', the large crowd supposed to inherit a new earth. The problem was that Jehovah's Witnesses in the beginning were not so numerous; they could therefore be fitted into a heaven restricted to the 144,000. But when the numbers of Witnesses increased and began to run into the millions, a solution had to be found for their salvation. Thus the solution of the 'other sheep' was invented in 1935.

The 'other sheep' (the Jonadab or large crowd class) are said not to be born again. They have no hope of going to heaven. If and when they pass a test of 1000 years and survive Armageddon, they will live in a secondary paradise: on earth. The doctrine contradicts Scripture teaching (see chapter 5), and was purely invented to solve an embarrassing hole in Watch Tower doctrine:

"The greatest insult to Jesus Christ comes from your telling millions that they cannot receive God's spirit to become his spiritual sons. You know very well that this undeserved kindness is offered to all who read the Word of God; and just because you thought that the number that could fit into heaven was filled, first in 1881, then 1918 and later 1935, you tell others that they will live on the earth and that it will take a 1000 years to make them perfect. Newcomers are intimidated from partaking in the Lord's memorial. You do not even admit that the 'other sheep' are technically Christians as you did before" (*Public Letter to the Governing Body* by Randall Watters, who worked in Brooklyn headquarters, dated January 22, 1981).

"This people honours me with their lips, but their heart is far from me. In vain do they worship me, teaching as doctrines the precepts of men" (Mark 7:6-7; Isaiah 29:13).

7.2 The Watchtower authorities proclaim prophecies and teachings they know to be untrue.

I will prove this by an assessment of one key prophecy in Watchtower doctrine, the one concerning the year 1914.

According to current Watchtower doctrine, the end of the world started in 1914. The so-called 'Gentile Times' ended, and Jesus Christ was put on a throne in heaven to 'rule in the midst of his foes' (Psalm 110:2). Because the 'end time' has now begun we can soon expect the end of the world.

Many Watchtower claims rest on the 1914 date. Jesus Christ, it is claimed, returned to earth in 1914, inspected Christian groups and, in 1919, appointed the Watchtower leaders to be his sole channel of communication to humankind. Christ's 'invisible presence' since 1914 has fulfilled the Scriptural texts announcing his Second Coming. The end of the world is near...

However, the 1914 prophecy and its related doctrine are a hoax. The Watchtower leadership knows this.

7.2.1 The 1914 calculations are based on a mistake that has been covered up

The calculation starts from Daniel 4:25 in which Daniel tells Nebuchadnezzar:

"You shall be driven from among men, and your dwelling shall be with the beasts of the field; you shall be made to eat grass like an ox, and you shall be wet with the dew of heaven, and seven times shall pass over you, till you know that the Most High rules the kingdom of men, and gives it to whom he will" (Daniel 4:25).

- The 'seven times' are interpreted as being addressed to the Gentiles.

- The expression 'a time' is interpreted as meaning '360 days', because 'two and a half times' (Revelation 12:14) are equated with '1260 days' (Revelation 12:8).

• *Seven* times are, therefore, equal to '2520 days'.

• Since a 'day' in Scripture is interpreted as a 'year'
(after Numbers 14:45; Ezekiel 4:6), '2520 days' equal
'2520 years'.

The calculation then jumps to Jesus' words about the fall of
Jerusalem:

*"They will fall by the edge of the sword, and be led captive
among all nations; and Jerusalem will be trodden down by
the Gentiles, until the times of the Gentiles are fulfilled"
(Luke 21:24).*

• The 'times of the Gentiles' are equated with the 'seven
times' in Daniel 4:25. They are thus reckoned to be a
duration of '2520 years'.

• Jesus' words are interpreted to indicate a period of time
since the Fall of Jerusalem under Nebuchadnezzar. **Since
this is taken to have happened in 606 BC, the 2520 years
should be calculated from then.**

• 2520 years from 606 BC takes us to: 1914 AD
(= 2520-606).

All these calculations, and the connections between them, are of
course entirely speculative. But even if we take them seriously -
for the sake of argument - they fail on one important link: the
date of the Fall of Jerusalem.

Charles Taze Russell the first Watchtower prophet, took his
calculations from Nelson Barbour, a Second Adventist, who
assumed that the fall of Jerusalem took place in 606 BC.

Therefore, Russell and Barbour jointly prophesied in 1877 that the year 1914 would be the end of the Gentile times. Because of all the emphasis laid on this date in the years leading up to it, and ever since, the date 1914 became an unshakable pillar in Jehovah's Witness chronology.

However, Barbour and Russell were wrong in dating the fall of Jerusalem to 606 BC. Historical evidence has now proved without any possible doubt that Jerusalem fell in 587 BC. The historical evidence for this is overwhelming. It rests on at least 15 separate arguments including: datings from Neo-Babylonian chronicles, historical records and royal inscriptions; cuneiform tablets; astronomical diaries by which Babylonian events can be given an absolute date; lunar eclipse texts; synchronism with contemporary Egyptian chronology. (For extensive details, see: Carl Olaf Jonsson, *The Gentile Times* Reconsidered, Commentary press, Atlanta 1986).

The implications of this for Jehovah's Witness chronology are enormous. With the revised date of the fall of Jerusalem, the "end of the Gentile times" and the Second Coming of Christ would have to take place 20 years later, namely in 1934 and not in 1914! It means that the original prophecies were wrong, since nothing happened in 1934, and that, if the new calculation was true, the rest of their chronology is all awry. The Watchtower organisation has responded by doggedly sticking to its 1914 date. Against the rest of the whole world, they keep maintaining that Jerusalem fell in 606 BC. As usual, the facts are being bent to fit their crooked interpretations.

"Leave them alone; they are blind guides. And if a blind man leads a blind man, both will fall into a pit" (Matthew 15:14).

7.2.2 The 1914 prophecies are totally unfulfilled

Ever since 1876, the Watchtower leaders began to prophesy the momentous events that were supposed to happen in 1914.

In 1876: "The seven times will end in AD 1914."

In 1889: "The Battle of Armageddon will end in 1914 with the complete overthrow of earth's present rulership".

In 1894: "We cannot change the 1914 dates. They are God's dates not ours. Bear in mind that the end of 1914 is not the date for the beginning but for the end of the time of trouble".

In 1914 itself: "The Gentile times ended in the autumn of 1914, and Jesus was enthroned as Jehovah's Representative in the Theocratic Government... The old heavens and earth having thus been disposed of, this wicked world, which has been in its 'time of the end' since 1914 will come to its final end".

In 1922: "Christ has returned in 1914, but he has done so 'invisibly'.

The Watchtower organisation had a stroke of good luck because the first world war started in 1914. This was claimed to be a fulfilment of the prophecy. Even today, in Watchtower literature, it is claimed that the beginning of the first world war has initiated a new era in human history. However, the same could be said of so many other dates. Surely, the second world war was much more devastating than the first ever was. Moreover, the detonation of the first nuclear bomb in 1945 was much more crucial than the start of the first world war in 1914. In spite of

Jehovah's Witness claims, 1914 was not much different from years that preceded or followed on.

The truth of the matter is that the real prophecies, about the ending of the Gentile Times, the Second Coming of Christ and the abolition of all temporary governments, and so on, have not materialised. The prophecy simply has not come true!

"Beware of false prophets, who come to you in sheep's clothing but inwardly are ravenous wolves. You will know them by their fruits" (Matthew 7:15).

7. 2. 3. The second coming of Christ will not be invisible

The Watchtower claims that Christ has returned to earth "invisibly" and has been given the world rulership "invisibly" since 1914. This contradicts the Scriptural message.

In Sacred Scripture the Second Coming of Christ is always presented as an earth shaking event that will be entirely visible.

"Men of Galilee, why do you stand looking into heaven? This Jesus, who was taken up from you into heaven, will come in the same way that you saw him go into heaven" (Acts 1:11).

"We who are alive, who are left until the coming of the Lord, shall not precede those who have fallen asleep. For the Lord himself will descend from heaven with a cry of command, with the archangel's call, and with the sound of trumpet of God" (1 Thessalonians 4:15-16).

"When the Son of Man comes as King and all the angels with him, he will sit on his royal throne and the people of all the nations will be gathered before him" (Matthew 25:31-32).

The contention that Jesus has returned "invisibly" is just

an excuse to cover up the failure of past prophecy. This cover up is perpetrated in spite of the unequivocal teaching of Sacred Scripture.

7.2.4. Hyped up "last day" expectations are proved wrong

Since 1914 was claimed to be the starting point of the "end time", it became a new yard stick to expect an imminent end of the world. The words of Jesus Christ, "truly I say to you that this generation will by no means pass away until all these things occur" (Matthew 24:34) were stated to apply from that year 1914.

In 1968 this claim was made: "Jesus was obviously speaking about those who were old enough to witness with understanding what took place when the 'last days' began. Jesus was saying that some of those persons who were alive at the appearance of the 'sign of the last days' would still be alive when God brought this system to its end. Even if we presume that youngsters 15 years of age would be perceptive enough to realise the import of what happened in 1914, it would still make the youngest of 'this generation' nearly 70 years old today. So the great majority of the generation to which Jesus was referring has already passed away in death. The remaining ones are approaching old age. And remember, Jesus said that the end of this wicked world would come before that generation passed away in death. This, of itself, tells us that the years left before the foretold end comes cannot be many..."

This was part of the hype up of the end of the world expectation prophesied for 1975. Of course, 1975 came and went, without the world having ended. As usual, the Watchtower twisted and bent its own words to somehow keep the imminent expectation of the end of the world intact. It was said the age limit of those witnessing the events in 1914, could be lowered. Later (in 1978 and 1980) it was stated that some people reach incredibly long ages, so that someone of 115 years old could still remember 1914...

Recently, the Watchtower has changed its tune. "We are not sure if any survivor of 1914 will be alive at the end of the world..."

"A faithful witness does not lie, but a false witness breathes out lies" (Proverbs 14,5).

"A truthful witness saves lives, but one who utters lies is a betrayer" (Proverbs 14,25).

7.2.5 The futility of trying to calculate the timing of the end of the world

A great folly implicit in all these stories is that the Watchtower organisation believes it can somehow, by extracting secret information from obscure Scripture texts, prophesy when key events of the last times will take place.

This attempt is, however, totally contrary to Scriptural teaching. Jesus Christ himself has constantly warned us that we will not know the exact time or the hour of his coming or of the end of the world.

"Of that day and hour no one knows, not even the angels of heaven, nor the Son, but only the Father" (Matthew 24:36).

"Watch, therefore, for you do not know on what day your Lord is coming" (Matthew 24:42).

"Therefore you also must be ready; for the Son of Man is coming at an hour you do not expect" (Matthew 24:44).

"Take heed, watch and pray; for you do not know when the time will come" (Mark 13:33).

"It is not for you to know the times or seasons which the Father has fixed by his own authority" (Acts 1:7).

7.3 The leaders of the Watchtower organisation usurp a spiritual authority that is not theirs

It is clear from the Gospels that Jesus Christ appointed twelve Apostles to whom he entrusted the task of preaching the Gospel (Matthew 10:1-42). To these Apostles Jesus gave authority (Matthew 18:18). On them he breathed his Spirit, so that they could forgive sins (John 20:23). To them he delegated his mission on the day he went up to heaven:

> *"All authority in heaven and on earth has been given to me. Go therefore and make disciples of all nations, baptising them in the name of the Father and of the Son and of the Holy Spirit, teaching them to observe all that I have commanded you; and, lo, I am with you always, to the close of the age" (Matthew 28:19).*

"I am with you always." With this Jesus indicated that he was not just speaking to the original Twelve, but to those who would succeed them in their ministry. From the earliest times onwards, the Apostles appointed others to help them and succeed them in their task. This is known as the apostolic succession (see Acts 14:23; 20:17, 28; etc.). The successors to the Apostles were bishops, elders (= priests) and deacons (1 Timothy 3:1-13; Titus 1:5-9; etc.).

The leaders of the Watchtower Society have no authority delegated to them by Christ. If, as they say, Christ appointed them in 1919 to be his sole channel of communication for humankind, what happened to all the centuries before? And how can they presume that Christ does not speak through the Christian bishops and priests who, in generation after generation, received the apostolic succession in the ministry?

Do the scriptural warnings not apply to them?

"Listen, the Lord has not sent you, and you have made this people trust in a lie. Behold, I will remove you from the face of the earth!" (Jeremiah 28:15-16).

Are they not corrupting the people they presume to teach?

"Woe to you, hypocrites! For you traverse land and sea to make a single proselyte, and when he becomes a proselyte, you make him twice as much a child of hell as yourselves" (Matthew 23:15).

Conclusion

Dear Jehovah's Witness, nobody doubts your sincere desire to submit to God and to share God's love and happiness in heaven. For the sake of your own salvation, leave the Watchtower organisation and return to your Christian roots.

In the established Christian community of saints you will rediscover that God is truly Love (1 John 4:8). The Father will receive you back with open arms (Luke 15:11-24). For you, too, like every other human being are invited to become an adopted child of God (John 1:12-13) and so to inherit the fulness of salvation with God in heaven.

"It is the Spirit himself bearing witness with our spirit that we are children of God, and if children, then heirs, heirs of God [the Father] and fellow heirs with Christ" (Galatians 8:16-17).